Catholic Update
guide to the
New
Evangelization

MARY CAROL KENDZIA,
Series Editor

Franciscan
MEDIA
Cincinnati, Ohio

RESCRIPT

In accord with the *Code of Canon Law*, I hereby grant my *Imprimatur*
the *Catholic Update Guide to the New Evangelization.*

Vicar General and Auxiliary Bishop
of the Archdiocese of Cincinnati
Cincinnati, Ohio
November 5, 2012

The *Imprimatur* ("Permission to Publish") is a declaration that a book or pamphlet is considered
to be free from doctrinal or moral error. It is not implied that those who have granted the
Imprimatur agree with the contents, opinions or statements expressed.

Cover and book design by Mark Sullivan
Cover image © Fotolia | Elnur

ISBN 978-1-61636-582-0

Printed in the United States of America.
Printed on acid-free paper.
13 14 15 16 17   5 4 3 2 1

Contents

About This Series

The Catholic Update guides take the best material from our best-selling newsletters and videos to bring you up-to-the-minute resources for your faith. Topically arranged for these books, the words you'll find in these pages are the same clear, concise, authoritative information you've come to expect from the nation's most trusted faith formation series. Plus, we've designed this series with a practical focus—giving the "what," "why," and "how to" for the people in the pews.

The series takes the topics most relevant to parish life—e.g., the Mass, sacraments, Scripture, the liturgical year—and draws them out in a fresh and straightforward way. The books can be read by individuals or used in a study group. They are an invaluable resource for sacramental preparation, RCIA participants, faith formation, and liturgical ministry training, and are a great tool for everyday Catholics who want to brush up on the basics.

The content for the series comes from noted authors such as Thomas Richstatter, O.F.M., Lawrence Mick, Leonard Foley, O.F.M., Carol Luebering, William H. Shannon, and others. Their theology and approach is grounded in Catholic practice and tradition, while mindful of current Church practice and teaching. We blend each author's style and approach into a voice that is clear, unified, and eminently readable.

Enrich your knowledge and practice of the Catholic faith with the helpful topics in the Catholic Update Guide series.

Mary Carol Kendzia
Series Editor

Introduction

"I give you a new commandment, that you love one another. Just as I have loved you, you also should love one another."

—John 13:34

The history of the Church can be charted against the backdrop of evangelization. Down through the past two thousand years, from the time Jesus lived on this earth, the Church has tried to meet the challenge of reaching out to others with the Good News of Jesus Christ.

Since the Second Vatican Council, the responsibility for evangelization has shifted from being solely the work of church officials, clergy, and religious communities—the pope, cardinals, bishops, priests, brothers, and religious sisters—to being an effort on the part of all faithful Catholics to better know Christ and reach out to their family, friends, community, and the world to communicate the love of God everyday in ways both small and big. This is the New Evangelization we speak of today.

The call to evangelization itself is not new. After the death of Jesus, the disciples and other followers listened to his command to "Go therefore and make disciples of all nations, baptizing them in the name of the Father and of the Son and of the Holy Spirit, and teaching them to obey everything that I have commanded you" (Matthew 28:19–20), taking the Good News to Asia, Africa, and Western Europe.

At the heart of evangelization is the Great Commandment: "'You shall love the Lord your God with all your heart, and with all your soul, and with all your mind, and with all your strength' ... 'You shall love your neighbor as yourself.' There is no other commandment greater than these" (Mark 12:30–31). This commandment would be the badge worn by followers of Jesus Christ; this is what would distinguish Christianity from all other faiths.

This new commandment is not a repudiation of the Ten Commandments. In the same way, the New Evangelization does not reject past evangelization efforts.

In *A Concise Guide to the Documents of Vatican II*, Edward P. Hahnenberg noted that, following Vatican II, "the older paradigm of missionary work that saw the European Church 'sending' and the rest of the world 'receiving' gave way to a new paradigm: a vision of the whole worldwide Church sharing together in the one mission of evangelizing the world."

This new paradigm is then one of the key elements meant by the phrase "New Evangelization," a phrase, as Hahnenberg notes, that was "first used by the bishops of Latin America gathered at Medellin (Columbia) in 1968," and then "lifted up by Pope John Paul II to become a hallmark of his papacy" and, more recently, encouraged and expanded by Pope Benedict XVI and the late 2012 Synod of Bishops on the subject.

"What makes the new evangelization 'new' is not the message—the good news of Jesus Christ remains the same always. Rather, it is new in approach, attitude and scope. It is an evangelization directed not to an unknown unbeliever in an unfamiliar corner of the world. Instead it is an evangelization directed to the whole world, its many cultures and its peoples, both those who have never heard of Christ and those who have heard the Good News but forgotten what it means to follow Christ. The New Evangelization includes not only initial proclamation and pastoral care, but also re-evangelization of those whose lives are no longer inspired by the Gospel."

The love of neighbor, the reaching out to those who never have known Christ or whose relationship with Jesus has waned, the participation of all, the transformation of people and social structures, the use of new media to share faith—these are elements of our call to the New Evangelization.

The *Catholic Update Guide to the New Evangelization* offers a brief walk through a topic that too often confuses Catholics and leaves them wondering what their role is in the new evangelization. It will examine what evangelization is and why it is important; the history of how it has been shaped, especially from the Second Vatican Council to the present; what is new about the New Evangelization; and how each of us can answer the call of our Lord and Savior, Jesus Christ, in a way that is personal, relevant, and powerful.

CHAPTER ONE

What Is Evangelization?

"Go therefore and make disciples of all nations, baptizing them in the name of the Father and of the Son and of the Holy Spirit, and teaching them to obey everything that I have commanded you"

—Matthew 28:19–20

What does the word evangelization mean to you? When we think of evangelization, some of the images that may spring to mind are priests in pulpits, revival tents, televangelists addressing packed football stadiums, or Jehovah's Witnesses going from door to door seeking to gain converts by persuasive words.

Yet it is a common error to restrict the meaning of evangelization to preaching.

Actually, many people are already evangelizing without knowing it: mom and dad teaching their children Gospel values by embodying them in their daily lives; Marian, the college librarian, by being friendly to students and listening to their problems; Ted, by writing his senator or representative to urge better housing for the poor; the nurse, by comforting a fearful patient; the Boy Scout leader, by counseling youth; the wife, by fighting world hunger through working in local food banks; or the husband, by working with a hospice house in his area. These people are all engaged in evangelization.

We don't want to belittle preaching the Gospel: In fact, we must learn to do it better and more boldly. But we must see that evangelization is so much more than that. To share our faith more effectively with today's world, we first of all have to get a clearer and richer understanding of evangelization.

The word comes from the Latin word *evangelium* (Greek, *euangelion*) meaning "good news" or "gospel." To evangelize therefore means to do the Gospel, to live it, to carry it out, as well as to proclaim it.

To live the Gospel, to challenge others by one's example and lifestyle, to uphold true values, to open people's hearts to the saving power of God, to build community, to struggle against injustice, to work for the transformation of society—these are all vital elements of the activity known as evangelization.

You and I are the instruments of God's saving action in the world. Our counseling or preaching or social programs or parenting—in a word, our human techniques—are not of themselves saving or transforming the world or ushering in God's kingdom. Faith, salvation, the conversion of the world, the accomplishing of God's plan is brought about by God, not by us—except as instruments of his saving power.

Consider what happened at Pentecost. The apostles were powerless to make disciples of all nations until they were filled with the Spirit and transformed into powerful instruments of God's plan. This is why we need to remember that "through the power of the Holy Spirit the Good News of Jesus is proclaimed and lived." God is the chief architect of evangelization.

What does this mean for us practically? It means that one of our first steps in promoting and implementing the Gospel must be openness to God's power through prayer and sacramental life. It means interior personal renewal. For a parish it may mean programs that will help deepen the spirituality of that community. It means the whole Christian community must renew its inner life, and its members must energize each other by sharing their faith and Jesus's Spirit. It means submitting ourselves as more willing instruments of God's explosive power. Indeed, the advance of God's kingdom is first of all God's gift.

God Calls Us to Evangelization

In *Catholic and Confident: Simple Steps to Share Your Faith*, Henry Libersat notes that, in the past, Catholic evangelization was considered primarily the work of priests and other religious. "These people brought God's love to foreign lands, including the Americas. That was good! These priests and religious—many of whom were martyred for their faith—did wonderful work and brought millions into the Church."

But today, he says, "God asks you, a layperson—young or old, married or single—to bring the Good News of salvation to everyone in your life: to your family, the people at work, and those you meet while shopping, sitting in your doctor's office, coaching sports, or standing outside church before and after Sunday Mass." By virtue of baptism marking our life as disciples of Christ, laypersons "have the right, duty, and power to tell people about salvation through Jesus Christ."

It is love of God and neighbor, rather than academic degrees, that brings people to Christ and his Church. All, Libersat stresses, are called to the great commission of Jesus to "go therefore and make disciples of all nations" (Matthew 28:19).

God's Agents

Many may find the word *evangelization* a bit scary, bringing to mind unsettling scenes of people shoving tracts in neighbors' faces, or shouting about God and fear and damnation, or people walking down the street and "preaching" through a bullhorn, or TV evangelists fleecing their viewers.

Effective evangelization, Libersat says, is not any of these things. There is no need for shouting, for casting fear upon the masses. True evangelization relies on God's love and the truth and power of his Word. It is both gentle and friendly. When we share our faith, Jesus is our model. He had compassion on the unbeliever. He met people on their own level, and he spoke their language—in parables and stories they could understand.

The way we can evangelize is solidly rooted in the way we live and relate to other people.

Libersat points to Larry Puccio, a plumber living in Pembroke Pines, Florida, who offers a good example of true Catholic evangelizing. He has been a Catholic his entire life, but when his wife converted to Catholicism, her enthusiasm and knowledge of Christ led him closer to God. He and Lynn are active at St. Edward, a parish committed to evangelization, especially of people in the pew. No surprise that Larry has picked up the "faith-sharing bug." And he shares his faith in a friendly and effective way.

"When I am out on a job," Puccio explains, "I pray for the opportunity to tell people about my faith in Christ and about our Church." At a customer's house he may see a picture of a scene from Europe or portraits of family members or of other persons important to the household. "I ask the owners about the pictures—'Were you in Europe?' Or, 'Is that your father?'—and we share a bit about our families and experiences. I'll mention how important my parish is to me and how faith in God has enriched my life. If they are open to further sharing, we go for it."

Libersat points to the great effect we already have on other people, how we already help them. But how can we incorporate that into the greatest help possible—bringing them to know Jesus Christ?

If our relationship with Jesus Christ is genuine, it will show. People will see us celebrate something wonderful with them, and at other times mourning with them in their grief or comforting them in times of hardship. Being a friend, one who empathizes and supports, is the first step in helping people discover the secret to your happiness—an intimate union with Jesus Christ, your Lord and Savior.

It's All About Jesus

When we share faith with others, we have to start with Jesus. He is the "blessed…one who comes in the name of the Lord" (Matthew 21:9), the one who reconciles us with the Father (see 2 Corinthians 5:18). He is the way into the joy and strength of faith, the truth that is God's love, and the life that restlessly seeks the heart of each and every person on earth.

God wants all people to be saved. He fills us with his Holy Spirit—to guide and inspire us, to give us insight, wisdom, and courage. In baptism we were marked with the priestly character of Christ himself.

We were called to do what Jesus did. The Second Vatican Council, in its Decree on the Apostolate of the Laity, summed it up in these words: "There are innumerable opportunities open to the laity for "exercising the apostolate of evangelization and sanctification. The very testimony of their Christian life and good works done in a supernatural spirit have the power to draw men to belief and to God, for the Lord says, 'Even so let your light shine so brightly before men in order that they may see your good works and give glory to your Father who is in heaven' (Matthew 5:16)."

It is crystal clear: We are called to do what Jesus did. We can and we must.

Why Evangelize?

The question remains: Why do we or should we evangelize?

First, according to David Thorp who wrote "Evangelizing as a Parish," which appears in *John Paul II and the New Evangelization* (Servant), we do so out of obedience to Jesus. He gave us and the Church, on the day of the Ascension, the continual task of evangelizing until all have heard his Good News and until every person from every nation has been made his disciples (see Matthew 28:19–20).

Second, we evangelize because we have become convinced that what we have to share is Good News—indeed, the best news. We echo the words of Peter when many of Jesus's disciples no longer followed him: "Lord, to whom can we go? You have the words of eternal life. We have come to believe and know that you are the Holy One of God" (John 6:68–69). We share the Gospel with others because salvation is offered to every person in Jesus Christ, because in him people can be brought enlightenment and be lifted from error.

Third, we evangelize because we are surrounded by people who are hungering, thirsting, and literally dying for the Good News in their lives. While they may not express their need, we know that many live in doubt, wondering to themselves: Is anyone there? Does anyone care? Is there hope? Is there any sense and meaning to life? Is life possible? If we have the answer to their questions—Jesus Christ—then to withhold the way, the truth and the life is to violate the rights of others and to place ourselves in peril, as Pope Paul VI pointed out in his apostolic exhortation *Evangelii Nuntiandi*.

Fourth, we evangelize because of love for others. As we have experienced Jesus's love, we want to share it. The gifts we have received from God are not gifts for us alone, but build in us a desire to bring all people to the Good News.

Questions for Reflection

1. How would you define authentic Catholic evangelism?
2. Why do you, as a layperson, have to be concerned with evangelization?
3. What are some ways you can begin to share the Good News with those around you?

CHAPTER TWO

The History of Evangelization in the Church

> "The moment has come to commit all of the Church's energies to a new evangelization and to the mission ad gentes. No believer in Christ, no institution of the Church, can avoid this supreme duty: to proclaim Christ to all peoples."
>
> —Pope John Paul II, *Redemptoris Missio:* On the Permanent Validity of the Church's Missionary Mandate

In looking at evangelization, the figure of St. Paul looms large. Paul is the most prominent personality of the New Testament, apart from Jesus himself. He is an important enough figure that Pope Benedict XVI proclaimed for the Church a special year to honor St. Paul the apostle in 2008, the two thousandth anniversary of his birth.

Thirteen of the twenty-seven books of the New Testament bear his name. All of them are letters. Much of what we know about Paul comes from these remarkable written sources, supplemented by stories from the Acts of the Apostles, in which Paul figures prominently in the second half (chapters 9—28).

Paul himself admits that he persecuted the Church out of zeal for his Jewish background. However, around the year 35 A.D. he had a remarkable experience. On the road to Damascus, the risen Lord, Jesus, appeared to him and called him to be "the apostle to the Gentiles" (see Acts 9:1–19).

Paul would not characterize his experience as a conversion in the sense of a change of religion, but more likely as a call or commission. Acts portrays the event in terms reminiscent of the call of Old Testament prophets, and this is consistent with Paul's own description found in Acts.

Paul considers himself an apostle, one who has been called and sent by the Lord Jesus himself for a special mission. He was to bring the Gentiles into the fold of those who accepted Jesus of Nazareth as the long-awaited Messiah, the Savior of the world.

After his call, Paul began an intense ministry of evangelization. He took up (or returned to) the work of tent making so that he would not be a burden to the communities he served. After a mysterious three-year period in Arabia, he went to Jerusalem to meet with Peter, James (the brother of the Lord) and John (in about 38 A.D.). They were leaders of the new movement of Jesus's followers in Jerusalem that Acts calls "the Way" and who eventually became known as "Christians."

These leaders apparently endorsed Paul's mission to the Gentiles. Paul, accompanied by colleagues, then went to Syria, Cilicia, and Galatia and eventually crossed over into Europe to proclaim the Gospel of Jesus Christ in Macedonia, Achaia, and throughout the Mediterranean region.

Acts portrays Paul's missionary activity in a series of three extensive journeys that show the expanding Christian mission in stages, going from Judea to Samaria to "the ends of the earth."

Paul's ministry was missionary evangelization, which he exercised with great effect. He established communities of faith in many major cities of the Roman Empire, such as Ephesus, Corinth, Philippi, and Thessalonica.

Vatican II Resurrects the Idea of Evangelization

According to Cardinal Avery Dulles, widely viewed as one of the leading U.S. Catholic theologians of the twentieth century, some historical developments over the past three hundred years "have gradually resuscitated the idea of evangelization."

"The progressive secularization of European and American culture…prevented the churches from relying as they previously had on political and sociological factors to maintain the faith," he wrote in an essay titled "Pope John Paul and the New Evangelization: What Does It Mean." "In the new pluralistic situation, faith increasingly became a matter of personal decision in response to the testimony of convinced believers."

Dulles pointed to Protestant evangelical revivals that began in the eighteenth century in England and the United States. For Catholicism, the twentieth century brought "an analogous evangelical renewal."

The Second Vatican Council marked, the cardinal noted, an important stage in this shift to be an evangelizing Church. "A simple word count indicates the profound shift in focus. Vatican I, which met from 1869 to 1879, used the term gospel (*evangelium*) only once and never used the terms evangelize or evangelization."

"Less than a century later," he noted, "Vatican II mentioned the gospel 157 times and used the verb evangelize 18 times and the noun evangelization 31 times." He pointed out that when the council spoke of evangelization, it "generally meant the proclamation of the basic Christian message of salvation through Jesus Christ."

Evangelization is the essence of the Church's identity, made clear by the Second Vatican Council document, On the Mission Activity of the Church (*Ad Gentes*), issued in 1965. "The pilgrim Church is missionary by her very nature, since it is from the mission of the Son and the mission of the Holy Spirit that she draws her origin, in accordance with the decree of God the Father."

Building on the council's work, Paul VI dedicated his pontificate to the task of evangelization. His choice of the name Paul signified his intention to take the proclaimed mission of St. Paul, the "apostle to the Gentiles," as the model of his papal ministry.

Called "the pilgrim pope," Paul VI was the first pontiff in history to make apostolic journeys to other continents, including pilgrimages to the Holy Land and India in 1964, to New York in 1965, to Portugal, Istanbul, and Ephesus in 1967, to Columbia in 1968, to Uganda in 1969, and then, in 1970, Iran, Pakistan, the Philippines, Western Samoa, Australia, Indonesia, Hong Kong, and Sri Lanka.

Wishing to more greatly involve the wider Church in the dissemination of the Gospel, Paul VI chose as the theme of the synod of bishops in 1974 "the evangelization of the modern world." In his great 1975 apostolic exhortation, *Evangelii Nuntiandi* (On Evangelization in the Modern World), he described evangelization as the "deepest identity" of the Church, which "exists in order to evangelize, that is to say in order to preach and teach, to be the channel of the gift of grace, to reconcile sinners with God, and to perpetuate Christ's sacrifice in the Mass, which is the memorial of his death and glorious Resurrection" (*Evangelii Nuntiandi*, 14).

The pope made it clear that there can be no evangelization without explicit proclamation of Jesus as Lord (*Evangelii Nuntiandi*, 22) and it cannot be reduced to any sociopolitical project of development and liberation (*Evangelii Nuntiandi*, 31–33).

The Call for a New Evangelization

Pope John Paul II carried this evangelical impetus yet further. He declared in Mexico City on May 6, 1990, that evangelization formed the center of his pontificate, just as Paul VI had.

The pontificate of John Paul II saw him make 105 foreign trips, including six to the United States. "The Lord and master of history and of our destinies has wished my pontificate to be that of a pilgrim pope of evangelization, walking down the roads of the world, bringing all peoples the message of salvation."

Beginning in 1983, the pope issued repeated calls for a "new evangelization." Evangelization, John Paul II stressed, cannot be new in its content, since its theme is always the one Gospel in Jesus Christ. If it arose as merely a human endeavor, he said, "it would not be 'gospel' but mere human invention, and there would be no salvation in it."

Evangelization, however, can and should be new in its methods and its expression. It must be proclaimed with new energy and in a style and language adapted to the people of our day.

In one of his major encyclicals, *Redemptoris Missio* (On the Permanent Validity of the Church's Missionary Mandate), John Paul II stated the importance of the Church not waiting to proclaim the Gospel. Christ's mission as redeemer, "which is entrusted to the Church, is still very far from completion," he said. "This mission is still only beginning and…we must commit ourselves wholeheartedly to its service."

The primary reason the Church engages in missionary activity is to issue an explicit call to conversion in Christ, John Paul II said in his eighth encyclical letter, released in December 1990 on the twenty-fifth anniversary of the Vatican II document, Decree on the Church's Missionary Activity.

The letter came when the Church stood on the brink of the third millennium and the observance of the five hundredth anniversary of the evangelization of the Americas, and it served to update the understanding of our missionary role as followers of Christ. "I sense that the moment has come to commit all of the Church's energies to a new evangelization and to the mission *ad gentes*. No believer in Christ, no institution of the Church, can avoid this supreme duty: To proclaim Christ to all peoples," the pope stressed.

John Paul II, quoting Vatican II, pointed the Church to the work of "missionary activity" as "the greatest and holiest duty of the Church," adding that "there is a new awareness that missionary activity is a matter for all Christians."

He noted that our times are filled with great challenges to evangelization, but that they also present great opportunities as "we have witnessed the collapse of oppressive ideologies and political systems; the opening of frontiers and the formation of a more united world due to an increase in communication, the affirmation among peoples of the Gospel values which Jesus made incarnate in his own life (peace, justice, brotherhood, concern for the needy); and a kind of soulless economic and technical development which only stimulates the search for the truth about God, about man and about the meaning of life itself.... God is opening before the Church the horizons of a humanity more fully prepared for the sowing of the Gospel."

In the encyclical, John Paul II urged the Church to draw upon witness as a way to "achieve this goal." "People today put more trust in witnesses than in teachers, in experience than in teaching, and in life and action than in theories. The witness of a Christian life is the first and irreplaceable form of mission: Christ, whose mission we continue, is the 'witness' par excellence (Revelation 1:5; 3:14) and the model of all Christian witness."

"The evangelical witness which the world finds most appealing is that of concern for people, and of charity towards the poor, the weak and those who suffer," he added. "A commitment to peace, justice, human rights and human promotion is also a witness to the Gospel when it is a sign of concern for persons and is directed towards integral human development."

John Paul II pointed to proclamation as "the permanent priority of mission.... The Church cannot elude Christ's explicit mandate, nor deprive men and women of the 'Good News' about their being loved and saved by God."

The pope directly faced the issue about the responsibility of the Church. "It is claimed that it is enough to help people to become more human or more faithful to their own religion, that it is enough to build communities capable of working for justice, freedom, peace and solidarity,'" he said. "What is overlooked is that every person has the right to hear the 'Good News' of the God who reveals and gives himself in Christ."

It is not enough to suggest that any faith choice is as good as another, the encyclical suggests. The Church must make clear its belief that "for all people—Jews and Gentiles alike—salvation can only come from Jesus Christ," it said.

"While acknowledging that God loves all people and grants them the possibility of being saved," the pope wrote, "the Church believes that God has established Christ as the one mediator and that she herself has been established as the universal sacrament of salvation."

All Christians have an obligation to witness to their faith and to support missionary activity. A person who accepts the call to be a missionary must be convinced that "true liberation consists in opening oneself to the love of Christ."

A renewed commitment to missionary activity would be good for what ails the Church, wrote John Paul II in the encyclical. "Only by becoming missionary will the Christian community be able to overcome its internal divisions and tensions and rediscover its unity and its strength of faith."

Essential Elements of the New Evangelization

According to Cardinal Avery Dulles, the Church's new understanding of evangelization follows the Vatican II call to preach the Gospel to the nations.

A key feature is "the active participation of the whole church," said the cardinal. "Every believer is required to take an active part."

Cardinal Dulles told a meeting of U.S. bishops in 1995 that there is great similarity between what has been widely discussed as the "New Evangelization" that John Paul II had repeatedly called for in the Church, and what Paul VI stressed in his 1975 apostolic exhortation, *Evangelii Nuntiandi*. He outlined seven essential and common elements of the New Evangelization, as spelled out by Paul VI and John Paul II, that make it different from the Church's understanding of missionary activity before the Second Vatican Council half a century ago:

1. It is "inclusive"—"the whole process whereby individual and social life are transformed in the light of the Gospel," involving continuing evangelization of believers and re-evangelization of

inactive believers as well as the traditional first missionary proclamation.

2. It involves "participation by all" instead of being reserved "to certain groups of clergy and religious."

3. It is based on "religious freedom," relying on the power of the Gospel itself to draw people and rejecting past models under which Christian missionaries sometimes used "moral or physical force" to bring about conversions.

4. It includes dialogue, not as a substitute for proclamation but along with it.

5. It seeks to bring the Gospel to many cultures, drawing out the best in each and transforming it with the Gospel, instead of bringing along just a European understanding of culture as if it were part of the Gospel.

6. It includes "transformation of social structures" as a constitutive element of preaching the Gospel, insisting on the primacy of the spiritual but not reducing the Church's task to saving "individual souls for eternal life."

7. It involves appropriate "use of new media" but avoids letting the Gospel be "curtailed or deformed" to suit the media.

"Go and Make Disciples"

Drawing upon the call of John Paul II that evangelization represents "the greatest and holiest duty of the Church," the U.S. bishops issued a document in 1992 titled "Go And Make

Disciples," with the subtitle "A National Plan and Strategy for Catholic Evangelization in the United States." This document was meant to encourage American Catholics to be enthusiastic about their faith and share it with others in a variety of ways.

"Go And Make Disciples" described a national vision of evangelization as having both inward growth and renewal—a re-evangelizing—and an outward call to those who had stopped practicing their faith or who had not heard the Gospel message. "We know that the word 'evangelization' sometimes raises uncomfortable images for Catholics—especially in the culture of the United States where evangelism has sometimes meant only an individual response to enthusiastic preaching, or a style of mass religion, or contrived ways to recruit new members, or, at its worst, a way to play on people's needs," the document said.

The document further said that evangelization should be a call to deepen understanding among practicing Catholics; re-evangelize those who are Catholic in name only; reconcile those who have stopped practicing their faith; form children into disciples; invite other Christians to know the Church's message; and call to conversion those who have no faith.

"While we acknowledge that the grace of God is mysteriously present in all lives, people all too often resist this grace," it continued. "They refuse change and repentance. We evangelize so that the salvation of Christ Jesus, which transforms our human lives even now, will bring as many as possible to the promised life of unending happiness in heaven."

The bishops expressed a desire to invite all of God's children to their place in the Church: "We want to let our inactive brothers and sisters know that they always have a place in the Church and that we are hurt by their absence—as they are...we want to help them see that, however they feel about the Church, we want to talk with them, share with them, and accept them as brothers and sisters."

"We have no reason to be shy about the heritage of our Catholic faith," the document says, encouraging Catholics to live out the Gospel personally but also to bring those values into the life of the United States, "affirming what is good, courageously challenging what is not."

"Seeing both the ideals and the faults of our nation, we Catholics need to recognize how much our Catholic faith, which has received so much from American culture, still has to bring to life in our country."

The Call to the New Evangelization Today

Pope Benedict XVI has continued the focus of John Paul II on the new evangelization. He has directed the Church to proclaim the Gospel not only to those who have not encountered Christ, but to those who have heard the Gospel. During his homily on June 28, 2010, the Solemnity of Sts. Peter and Paul, at the Basilica of

St. Paul Outside the Walls, Benedict XVI renewed the Church's call to the New Evangelization.

The pope noted that the New Evangelization is not new in its content but rather in its thrust and in its methods: "'New' not in the contents, but in the interior impulse, open to the grace of the Holy Spirit who constitutes the force of the new law of the Gospel and who always renews the Church; 'new' in the search of ways that correspond to the force of the Holy Spirit and are adapted to the times and the situations; 'new' because necessary also in countries which have already received the proclamation of the Gospel."

Benedict XVI called for the *riproporre* ("re-proposing") of the Gospel to those regions "still awaiting a first evangelization" and to those regions where the roots of Christianity are deep but have experienced "a serious crisis" of faith due to debilitating effects of secularization.

The pope sees that the Church must evangelize by entering into dialogue with modern culture and confronting the cultural crisis brought on by the secularization of this culture. To that end he established the Pontifical Council for the Promotion of the New Evangelization on September 21, 2010, and proposed that the New Evangelization be the focus of the next Synod of Bishops.

Benedict XVI noted that the Church is facing "the challenges of the present age [which] are certainly beyond human capacities;

they are the historical and social challenges, and with greater reason, the spiritual challenges…a more profound hunger, which only God can satiate." "Man of the third millennium," the pope said, "desires an authentic and full life, he has need of truth, of profound liberty, of gratuitous love. Also in the deserts of the secularized world, man's soul thirsts for God, for the living God." But, he added, "the process of secularization has produced a grave crisis of the sense of the Christian faith and of belonging to the Church."

Benedict XVI has also indicated that the New Evangelization is not a single formula meant for all circumstances; first and foremost, he stresses, it is a personal "profound experience of God."

In the working document for the world synod of bishops on the New Evangelization in October 2012, the Vatican echoed the pope's sentiment that Catholics who act like their faith has nothing to do with daily life are a significant impediment to the Church's ability to proclaim faith in Jesus Christ to the world. "Every one of the Church's actions has an essential evangelizing character and must never be separated from the duty to help others encounter Christ in faith," it said in the document titled, "The New Evangelization for the Transmission of the Christian Faith."

Benedict XVI had called the synod to respond to a situation where, "because of a lack of faith, various particular churches are witnessing a decline in sacramental and Christian practice among the faithful to the point that some members can even be called 'nonbelievers,'" the document said.

The document pointed to the Second Vatican Council as the source of the idea of "renewing the Church's evangelizing activity" in an effort to "respond to a sense of disorientation experienced by Christians facing powerful changes and divisions which the world was experiencing at that time." In the face of possible "pessimism or resignation," the Church looks to evangelization as a way to tap "the regenerating power of the universal call to salvation, desired by God for each individual," it said.

As such, this fundamental work of the Church is not just one program, initiative, or activity among others, but rather "the duty of all baptized Christians" to enable the Church "to respond to the universal call to holiness."

In evaluating signs that call for a renewed evangelization of the baptized, the working document cited: "a weakening of faith in Christian communities, a diminished regard for the authority of the magisterium, an individualistic approach to belonging to the Church, a decline in religious practice and a disengagement in transmitting the faith to new generations."

The document said cultural changes, especially secularization—accelerated and spread by globalization and greater access to media—are creating a situation in which many people see faith as unimportant, old fashioned, or simply irrelevant to modern life. At the same time, it said, more and more people show signs of despair, selfishness, loneliness, and a lack of purpose in life.

According to the synod document, faith in Jesus Christ brings the joy, enthusiasm, hope, and love people need to live better lives. It pointed to "Jesus himself, the Good News of God," as the first and greatest evangelizer. "He revealed himself as being sent to proclaim the fulfillment of the Gospel of God, foretold in the history of Israel, primarily through the prophets, and promised in Sacred Scripture."

For Jesus, evangelization is the way to draw people into an intimate relationship with the Father and the Spirit, it said. "This is the primary reason for his preaching and miracles: to proclaim a salvation which, even though manifested through concrete acts of healing, is not meant to indicate a desire for social or cultural change but a profound experience, accessible to each person, of being loved by God and learning to recognize him in the face of a loving and merciful Father."

The Church, it said, should see in the example of Jesus his "method of evangelizing," welcoming everyone and never excluding anyone: "First, the poor, then the rich like Zacchaeus and Joseph of Arimathea; outsiders like the centurion and the Syro-Phoenician woman; the righteous, like Nathanael; and prostitutes and public sinners with whom he also sat at table."

"Jesus knew how to plumb the depths of a person and elicit faith in the God who first loved us, whose love always precedes us and is not dependent on our own merits, because he is love itself," the document stressed. "He sets down how the Church is to evangelize, demonstrating for her the heart of the Christian faith, namely, to believe in love and in the face and voice of this love, namely, Jesus Christ."

When faith effectively transforms people's lives, it said, the results are "families which are a true sign of love, sharing and a hope which is open to life; communities equipped with a true ecumenical spirit; the courage to support initiatives for social justice and solidarity; and the joy of giving one's life to the priesthood or the consecrated life."

The document said a major challenge to the New Evangelization is the growing idea that faith is opposed to freedom and that the Church's claims to know what is true are suspect or even dangerous. It noted that many people today show "a widespread disorientation, which leads to forms of distrust of all that has been passed down about the meaning of life and to an unwillingness to adhere in a total, unconditional manner to what has been revealed as the profound truth of our being."

While many Catholics who question the Church's claims of truth may continue to do good works, without the strength of faith and the support of the Christian community, their good works are bound to weaken over time and their activity will lose its power to bring others to Christ. One of the most effective ways to show people how faith brings true freedom, according to the document, is through "the witness-value" of devoting one's life to the "lonely, marginalized or rejected, precisely because the face of Christ is reflected in these people."

"Evangelization consists in proposing the Gospel which transforms the human individual, his world and his personal story," it said. "This experience of the newness of the Gospel transforms every person," noting that today we can see the truth of the power of God's word through "extraordinary examples of courage, dedication, boldness, intuition and reason in the Church's work of bringing the Gospel to every person...on every continent."

Called to Witness

The U.S. bishops have renewed their call to the New Evangelization, urging Catholics at all levels in the Church to invite Catholics who have stopped practicing their faith to begin to do so once again.

Whether members of the hierarchy, priests and other parish workers, or laity, all Catholics must reach out "to our missing brothers and sisters...touch the lives of others, interact with them, and show them how the faith answers the deepest questions and enriches modern culture," they wrote in the 2012 document from the committee on evangelization and catechesis, titled "Disciples Called to Witness: The New Evangelization." According to this document, "The New Evangelization is a call to each person to deepen his or her own faith, have confidence in the Gospel, and possess a willingness to share the Gospel."

Referring to a study of inactive Catholics prepared by the Center for Applied Research in the Apostolate (CARA) at Georgetown University, the 11,000-word document pointed to estimates that less than one quarter—23 percent—of U.S. Catholics attend Mass each week. That 77 percent who are absent from Sunday liturgy "are not strangers: They are our parents, siblings, spouses, children and friends."

The bishops noted that many Catholics do not attend the celebration of the Eucharist because "they (1) have busy schedules or a lack of time, (2) have family responsibilities, (3) have health problems or disabilities, (4) have conflicts with work, (5) do not believe missing Mass is a sin, or (6) believe that they are not very religious people."

Quoting from their document, *Go and Make Disciples*, the bishops noted that some Catholics "were never formed in the faith after their childhood. Some have drifted away because of one issue or another. Some feel alienated from the Church because of the way they perceive the Church or its teaching. Some have left because they were mistreated by church representatives."

The document cites secularism, materialism, and individualism in contemporary society as contributing factors for lack of Mass attendance by U.S. Catholics. "The New Evangelization is a call to each person to deepen his or her own faith, have confidence in the Gospel, and possess a willingness to share the Gospel."

"The New Evangelization provides the lens through which people experience the Church and world around them," it added. "The New Evangelization invites people to experience God's love and mercy through the sacraments, especially through the Eucharist and penance and reconciliation."

The tie of evangelization to the parish is key, the bishops note, as it is through the local Catholic faith community that "one becomes engaged…learns how to become a disciple of Christ, is nurtured by Scripture, is nourished by the sacraments, and ultimately becomes an evangelizer."

It also points to discipleship, a commitment to the Christian life, active parish life, the liturgical life of the Church, the Christian family, and religious experience as among the ways to draw Catholics back to their faith.

"The New Evangelization does not seek to invite people to experience only one moment of conversion but rather to experience the gradual and lifelong process of conversion: to draw all people into a deeper relationship with God, to participate in the sacramental life of the Church, to develop a mature conscience, to sustain one's faith through ongoing catechesis, and to integrate one's faith into all aspects of one's life," the document said.

The bishops stress that the call to the New Evangelization is not an option, but rather a commandment from Christ to all Christians "to be his witnesses to the ends of the earth. We are to proclaim his Good News to all people, everywhere and at all times."

"How often," the bishops ask, "do we fail to realize that we are called to be Christ's witnesses to the world? Do we realize that our Baptism, Confirmation, and reception of the Eucharist bestow on us the grace we need to be disciples? Are we... inviting those around us to experience Christ's love and mercy through the Church? How often do we reach out to our missing brothers and sisters by inviting them to join us at Mass or by asking why they no longer feel welcomed at the Lord's Table?"

"The answers to these questions," they stress, "underlie the evangelizing mission of the Church, especially in the call of the New Evangelization."

The focus of the New Evangelization is an invitation to men and women living in today's world and culture into a personal and direct relationship with Jesus Christ and his Church. "The New Evangelization strives," in the bishops' words, "to engage our culture and to help us draw our inspiration from the Gospel."

"The New Evangelization is a call to each person to deepen his or her own faith, have confidence in the Gospel, and possess a willingness to share the Gospel. It is a personal encounter with the person of Jesus, which brings peace and joy."

Questions for Reflection

1. St. Paul considered himself called by Jesus as an apostle on a special mission. What is the special mission to which Jesus is calling you?

2. What are the seven essential elements of the New Evangelization that make it different from the Church's past missionary outreach? Discuss how these can be expressed in daily life.

3. Pope John Paul II stressed the importance of witnessing our faith. When have you been a witness to your faith or seen others witness theirs? How did you feel about this?

CHAPTER THREE

Go Out Into the World

"The New Evangelization is a call to each person to deepen his or her own faith, have confidence in the Gospel, and possess a willingness to share the Gospel. It is a personal encounter with the person of Jesus, which brings peace and joy."

—"Disciples Called to Witness:
The New Evangelization"

Over the last fifty years—from the Second Vatican Council through the pontificates of Paul VI, John Paul II, and Benedict XVI—the Church has proclaimed the coming of the kingdom as God's gift and, most importantly, our task. We cannot sit on the sidelines or hibernate before our TVs and claim: If God is the main champion of evangelization, then our own individual efforts are unimportant.

Nor can we hide behind the false notion that evangelization is the duty chiefly of bishops, priests, religious brothers and sisters, or parish leaders. As John Paul II stressed, there is not one single Christian who can exempt himself or herself from the task of bearing witness to the Gospel. Our baptism launches us into that role.

Opportunities for us to evangelize abound. Whether we volunteer to be a lay minister, to coach a parish team, visit the sick, help with the census, promote voter registration, go to the Peace Corps or the missions, or care for our families, we each have great evangelizing potential. We cannot see the Church's mission as restricted to foreign lands or the crossing of oceans.

Evangelization is needed wherever Gospel values have not been fully established. All we have to do is see the regular news coverage of how desperately our own society and institutions need to be evangelized—not to mention our own hearts. We must begin implementing the Gospel on our own turf.

We need to be more aware of the power of our good example and our personal contacts—even something as seemingly insignificant as our smile. Perhaps dioceses and parishes could perform a greater service by updating us on the full meaning of evangelization and training us to better use our potential.

No human being can say, "I'm incapable of communicating

God's love and healing to others." We can all transmit God's goodness to the world, and this is the essence of evangelization. Jesus best communicated God's love to the world not only by preaching, but even more so by the fulfillment of his mission to serve, heal, defend the oppressed, and lay his life down in love.

It is our daily loving service to others (and this includes our own families as well as strangers) that best reveals the Good News of God's kingdom. It doesn't matter whether you are a psychologist or a bartender, a teacher or an airline stewardess, you can convey a living experience of Christ to others when your service to them is warm, joyful, kind, and loving. This is evangelization at its best.

As Paul VI indicated in *Evangelii Nuntiandi*, such activity is part of our evangelizing mission: "The Church has the duty to proclaim the liberation [from hunger, poverty, injustice] of millions of human beings...the duty of assisting the birth of this liberation, of giving witness to it, of ensuring that it is complete. This is not foreign to evangelization."

Of course, as the pope himself warned, we should not forget the human heart as the primary focus of liberation and evangelization, for personal sin and selfishness are the root causes of these social evils. Without a doubt the deepest liberation of all is that of Christ setting men and women free from sin.

But side by side with the call to liberate the human heart from sin is our mission to eradicate from human society its "sinful structures"—namely, such institutionalized evils as the unequal distribution of food and wealth, racism, sexism, discrimination, unfair trade laws, and oppressive situations of all kinds. We must struggle against these things, for they are nothing else than the external expression of sin and obstacles to the full human development intended for us by God.

Respect Other Faiths and Traditions

When working among or interacting with the unchurched and those of other religious traditions, we should approach them with a deep sense of respect for the profound goodness and value they have in God's sight. We must rid ourselves of any smug, triumphant attitude that sees them as godless, in any way "less holy" than ourselves, devoid of religious values, or in which we see ourselves as the sale possessors of the truth. The Bible teaches that God's truth and Spirit are present everywhere. We must listen for his revelation in others and not assume that truth is a one-way street—with traffic flowing only from us to them.

The kingdom of God is an older and broader reality than the Church. Wherever people pray and open themselves to the mystery beyond them, wherever they love and forgive each other, live humbly and justly, the kingdom is somehow present among them, and the Word of God has come into their midst, even if they have not heard of Christ or his Church.

Hopefully, when the time is ripe, they will be drawn into the

Church, which our faith sees as the ideal visible manifestation of the kingdom. In the meantime we do not have to place them outside the scope of God's redemptive presence, known in the Bible as the kingdom.

We will be more effective in sharing our faith with the unchurched and those of other religions if we respect and know their customs, their language, their needs, their values, and their social attitudes and if we come to listen as well as to talk.

As members of a parish or Christian community, our love and concern should go out to every person there, not simply to our fellow Catholics. We should make a greater effort to be a loving neighbor to the unchurched and those of other faiths on our street or where we work or shop or go to school. We should be eager to serve their needs, offer them hospitality, and be ready to share our values and convictions with them.

We have so much in common with Christian brothers and sisters of other communions. Generally speaking, we enjoy the same Word of God with them, the same values, and indeed the same Spirit of Jesus. We need to discover and celebrate more often the union we do have with them. Divisions among us fracture the unity of God's kingdom and make his word less attractive to those who as yet do not accept the Gospel.

We need to pray more often with other Christians, study and share our common Scriptures with them, join in more ecumenical ventures as well as outreach programs to the unchurched, and help manage social justice projects. Since ignorance fosters bigotry and mistrust, we must learn more about each other's beliefs and practices and personal lives.

The Church invites or repels others by everything it says and does. Our activities as a community on behalf of justice, our presence in the civic community, our lifestyles as individuals and as a Church, and even our church buildings and liturgical style communicate an understanding of the Gospel.

If our Church is seen as an agent of peace and reconciliation in the world, if we are truly a symbol of hospitality and joyful service to others and form a loving community among ourselves, people will be attracted to join us. We must be a collective sign of God's goodness, openness, and acceptance to all men and women. We must present an inviting image to the world.

Sharing Your Story

Evangelization is calling people to Jesus Christ. It is a process of sharing what God has done in our lives.

Henry Libersat, author of *Catholic and Confident*, said that evangelization is not first about calling people into our sacramental life or teaching them the doctrines of the Church. That comes later, he said, after the person has become interested in the hope and joy offered in a life of faith in Christ.

Our own holiness is the best "gospel of freedom" we can offer, he stressed. If we are holy and happy, people will know we are somehow different, and they will want what we have. Then we can tell them how God has worked in our lives and how our faith community has helped us continue in our faith journey with the Lord in peace and harmony.

Libersat points us to consider that it is our own personal experience with God's saving love and the stories of other people we know that are the essential and foundational messages that will bring people to Christ. Tell others how we experienced conversion to Christ or how God's love saved our child or how his grace saw us through a terrible ordeal, such as the death of a loved one. People discover hope when they hear how God has helped you kick drug addiction, face a particularly difficult challenge or overcome resentment, anger, or fear.

While we can know that it is our personal witness of God's presence and activity in our lives that is important, how do we tell our story in a way that is effective and reaches others? Libersat offers several things to consider.

- First, it is important that evangelizers develop and embrace an attitude of "grateful repentance." God has been merciful to us: We have had times of feeling unloved or discouraged or fearful—and we are perpetually grateful that Jesus is merciful and thus did lift us out of the mud. His love propels us to share his goodness and passionate love with others.

• Second, continuously grow in your relationship with the Lord. If you are a committed disciple of Christ, you pray every day, attend Mass and receive the sacraments, live a moral life, and embrace all the truths the Church teaches. This keeps us in touch with the Lord and equips us for the mission of bringing people to the Father.

• Third, think about how to tell your story. What was going on in your life before you came to know the Lord? You don't have to specify your sins—it's enough to say you were totally disoriented, unable to make sense out of life, in stressful family relationships, or what have you. What led you to ask Jesus into your life? Was it your spouse, a child, a pastor, a friend, a religious program on TV?

• Fourth, describe how you experienced God's love. Was it a feeling of great warmth, a sudden sense of well-being, or new hope, peace, joy?

• Fifth, examine how your life has changed. What has happened in your relationships? Has your prayer life changed? Are you truly a happier person? Do people acknowledge the change in you?

• Finally, share your story conversationally. You are not preaching or teaching. You are giving humble and grateful witness to God's great action in your life. Be yourself. Truth whispered is louder than shouts.

Remember, evangelization is rooted in good relationships—with friends, coworkers, and people we meet every day. We are not in the numbers game. We want to help people discover the love and mercy of God right where they are.

Announcing the Kingdom

St. Paul instructed Bishop Timothy: "Proclaim the message; be persistent whether the time is favorable or unfavorable" (2 Timothy 4:2). We must stand for the Gospel and share God's love whether it is convenient or inconvenient, "favorable or unfavorable." We must do so gently and humbly, with kindness and respect for the dignity and conscience of the other person.

Look for opportunities to share what God has done for you—how he has healed you or helped you make an important decision. Tell people how God has blessed you with a good family, a loving spouse, a roof over your head, and food on the table. (Strange, but many people seem to forget that God does indeed provide these basic and common blessings.)

Or perhaps your marriage and family life have been a rough, painful experience. In that event share how God has helped you through the tough times. Whom did he put in your life to help you? In what ways did he manifest his love for you? How did you get free of anger and resentment?

Pray each day for God to lead you to someone with whom you can share your faith. Often you can pray with the person. Thank God for the gift of this person. Praise him for his goodness. Ask God to let his healing love flow. Ask him to forgive both of you your sins and to strengthen you in your weaknesses.

Pray for God's will to be done and for the courage, faith, and strength to accept and to live in his will. Then encourage the person to trust God and to depend on him; to seek his will, his strength, and his grace, even and especially if you feel he delays in answering the prayer.

Questions for Reflection

1. Is there someone in your life who demonstrates the qualities of a lay Catholic evangelist? Name a few of these qualities and how they affect others.

2. Think about your personal faith story. What are the key elements you could share with other people? What can you share about your own struggles that might encourage them in the faith?

3. What is the most important thing you have learned from this book about the process of evangelization?

Evangelization Checklist

Here is a list of questions for evaluating our evangelizing efforts. It can be used by individuals or by organizations.

1. Do we see God as the primary agent of evangelization? Does our approach—openness to God, prayer, good liturgy, spirit of renewal—demonstrate our belief that it is God's power and not simply our technique or effort which is transforming and saving the world?

2. Do we see evangelization as everyone's responsibility? Do we see responsibility residing chiefly in a few leaders (priests, sisters, brothers, and official mission agencies) or essentially in each and every member of the Church?

3. Do we communicate God's love? Do the people we relate to (especially the unchurched) experience us as warm, cheerful, compassionate mediators of God's goodness and saving love?

4. Is total human betterment part of our mission? Have we assimilated the Church's growing awareness of the link between evangelization and human liberation? What programs for social betterment have we undertaken for those we minister to?

5. Do we respect other traditions? When dealing with people of other beliefs, do we affirm their basic goodness as created in God's image? Do we seek to learn from them? Do we respectfully study their language, their cultural heritage, their values? Do we judge them by their standards (insight) or merely by our own (insult)?

6. Does our love go beyond Catholic borders? Is the parish community and each parish member truly concerned about every person in the parish territory and not only the Catholics?

7. Is our approach ecumenical? Have we taken the time to discover and celebrate what we share in common with those of other traditions? In what ways have we taken part and helped create or build common and cooperative ventures between faith groups: weeks of prayer for Christian unity, pulpit exchange programs, ecumenical prayer groups (exploring our common Scriptures), interfaith study groups, and social-action projects?

8. How are we using media today? How are we making effective use of methods of communications, whether television, movies, radio, newspapers, magazines, bulletins, CDs, audio or video downloads, Facebook or Twitter, among the many media sources that come into our lives daily? Are we sharing with others good news that reflects Gospel values of the Good News, or are we more involved with sharing with and promoting to others the interaction with the salacious or negative?

9. Do we fully utilize existing groups? Have we explored and affirmed the strengths of existing parish organizations and considered how their evangelizing roles can be intensified?

10. What is our total image? What do we as individuals or as a community convey to the unchurched or the Catholic who is away from the Church? What do we communicate in terms of our presence in the civic community, our lifestyles, the buildings themselves? How inviting is our parish by everything it says and does?

Sources

Committee on Evangelization and Catechesis, U.S. Conference of Catholic Bishops. "Disciples Called to Witness: The New Evangelization," 2012. Available at http://www.usccb.org/beliefs-and-teachings/how-we-teach/ new-evangelization/disciples-called-to-witness/ upload/Disciples-Called-to-Witness-5-30-12.pdf.

Dulles, Cardinal Avery, S.J. "Pope John Paul and the New Evangelization: What Does It Mean?" in Ralph Martin and Peter Williamson, eds. *John Paul II and the New Evangelization* (Cincinnati: Servant, 2006), pp. 2–16.

Hahnenberg, Edward P. *A Concise Guide to the Documents of Vatican II*. (Cincinnati: St. Anthony Messenger Press, 2007).

———. "Treasures of Vatican II: Our Compass for the Future." *Catholic Update*, September 2005.

Libersat, Henry. *Catholic and Confident: Simple Steps to Share Your Faith* (Cincinnati: Servant, 2012).

Pope John Paul II. *Redemptoris Missio*: On the permanent validity of the Church's missionary mandate, December 7, 1990. Available at http://www.vatican.va/holy_father/john_paul_ii/encyclicals/documents/hf_jp-ii_enc_07121990_redemptoris-missio_en.html.

————. "The Mission of Christ the Redeemer: Key Passages of Pope John Paul II's *Redemptoris Missio*: On the Permanent Validity of the Church's Missionary Mandate." *Catholic Update*, October 1991.

Pope Paul VI. *Evangelii Nuntiandi*, December 8, 1975. http://www.vatican.va/holy_father/paul_vi/apost_exhortations/documents/hf_p-vi_exh_19751208_evangelii-nuntiandi_en.html.

Thorp, David. "Evangelizing as a Parish," in Ralph Martin and Peter Williamson, eds. *John Paul II and the New Evangelization: How You Can Bring the Good News to Others* (Cincinnati: Servant, 2006), pp. 250–263.

U.S. Conference of Catholic Bishops. "Go and Make Disciples: A National Plan and Strategy for Catholic Evangelization in the United States," 1992 (rev. 2002). Available at http://www.usccb.org/beliefs-and-teachings/how-we-teach/evangelization/go-and-make-disciples/go-and-make-disciples-a-national-plan-and-strategy-for-catholic-evangelization-in-the-united-states.cfm.

Vatican, "The New Evangelization for the Transmission of the Christian Faith," May 27, 2012. Available at http://www.vatican.va/roman_curia/synod/documents/rc_synod_doc_20120619_instrumentum-xiii_en.html

Wintz, Jack, O.F.M. "How to Share Your Faith Today: A Short Course for Modern Evangelizers." *Catholic Update*, July 1977.

Witherup, Ronald D., S.S. "Introducing St. Paul the Apostle: His Life and Mission." *Catholic Update*, July 2008.

Contributors

Cardinal Avery Dulles, S.J., was a professor of religion and society at Fordham University, the author of twenty-seven books and over eight hundred articles, a lecturer and an elder statesman of Catholic theology in America. He was the only American theologian ever appointed to the college of cardinals, named by Pope John Paul II in 2001. Cardinal Dulles served as president of the Catholic Theological Society of America and of the American Theological Society. His books include *Models of the Church, The Reshaping of Catholicism* and *The Splendor of Faith: The Theological vision of Pope John Paul II.*

Edward P. Hahnenberg, is the author of *A Concise Guide to the Documents of Vatican II* and *Ministries: A Relational Approach.* He teaches theology at Xavier University in Cincinnati.

Henry Libersat is the author of sixteen books, including the international bestseller *Miracles Do Happen* (coauthored with Sr. Briege McKenna). He has a master's degree in pastoral ministry from St. Thomas University in Miami and was ordained a permanent deacon for the Orlando diocese in 1986. He and his wife,

Peg, have raised seven children and are now enjoying their many grandchildren.

David M. Thorp was the director of the Boston Archdiocese initiative Catholics Come Home, the Office of Charismatic Renewal Services, and the Office of Evangelization. He also served on the National Service Committee for the Catholic Charismatic Renewal and traveled nationally to provide support for Catholic prayer groups throughout the Northeast and organized annual conferences for national and local leaders as well as serving as the assistant director of the Spiritual Life Center of Marian Community in Medway, Massachusetts.

Jack Wintz, O.F.M., is the senior editor of *Catholic Update* and editor emeritus of *St. Anthony Messenger* magazine. The Franciscan friar is the author of Friar Jack's E-Spirations, *Will I See My Dog in Heaven?, St. Anthony of Padua: His Life, Legends, and Devotions,* and *Friar Jack's Favorite Prayers.*

Ronald D. Witherup, S.S., is provincial of the Sulpician Fathers, former Professor of Sacred Scripture at St. Patrick Seminary, Menlo Park, California, a prolific author, and a frequent contributor to American Catholic Radio. He is the author of *St. Paul: Called to Conversion: A Seven-Day Retreat.*